## Dinosaurs and Prehistoric Animals
# Giant Rhinoceros

by Janet Riehecky

Consulting Editor: Gail Saunders-Smith, PhD

Consultant: Jack Horner, Curator of Paleontology
Museum of the Rockies
Bozeman, Montana

Capstone
press

Mankato, Minnesota

Pebble Plus is published by Capstone Press,
151 Good Counsel Drive, P.O. Box 669, Mankato, Minnesota 56002.
www.capstonepress.com

1 2 3 4 5 6 14 13 12 11 10 09

*Library of Congress Cataloging-in-Publication Data*
Riehecky, Janet, 1953–
     Giant rhinoceros / by Janet Riehecky.
     p. cm. — (Pebble plus. Dinosaurs and prehistoric animals)
     Summary: "Simple text and illustrations present prehistoric giant rhinoceros, how they looked,
and what they did" — Provided by publisher.
     Includes bibliographical references and index.
     ISBN-13: 978-1-4296-0037-8 (hardcover)
     ISBN-10: 1-4296-0037-3 (hardcover)
     1. Rhinoceroses, Fossil — Juvenile literature. 2. Indricotherium — Juvenile literature. I. Title.
QE882.U6R54 2009
599.66'8 — dc22                                                    2006102210

**Editorial Credits**
Sarah L. Schuette and Jenny Marks, editors; Gene Bentdahl, designer; Wanda Winch, photo researcher

**Illustration and Photo Credits**
Jon Hughes, illustrator
Museum of Paleontology named after Y.A. Orlov, Paleontological Institute of the Russian Academy of Sciences,
     Moscow, Russia, 21

## Note to Parents and Teachers

The Dinosaurs and Prehistoric Animals set supports national science standards
related to the evolution of life. This book describes and illustrates the giant rhinoceros. The
images support early readers in understanding the text. The repetition of words and phrases
helps early readers learn new words. This book also introduces early readers to subject-specific
vocabulary words, which are defined in the Glossary section. Early readers may need assistance
to read some words and to use the Table of Contents, Glossary, Read More, Internet Sites, and
Index sections of the book.

# Table of Contents

# The Largest Mammals

Giant rhinoceroses were
the largest mammals
ever to walk the earth.

Giant rhinos lived

in prehistoric times.

They lived in Asia

about 30 million years ago.

# How Giant Rhinos Looked

Giant rhinos looked

like giraffes.

They grew up to 23 feet

(7 meters) tall.

Giant rhinos walked

on four long legs.

Their feet had hard hooves.

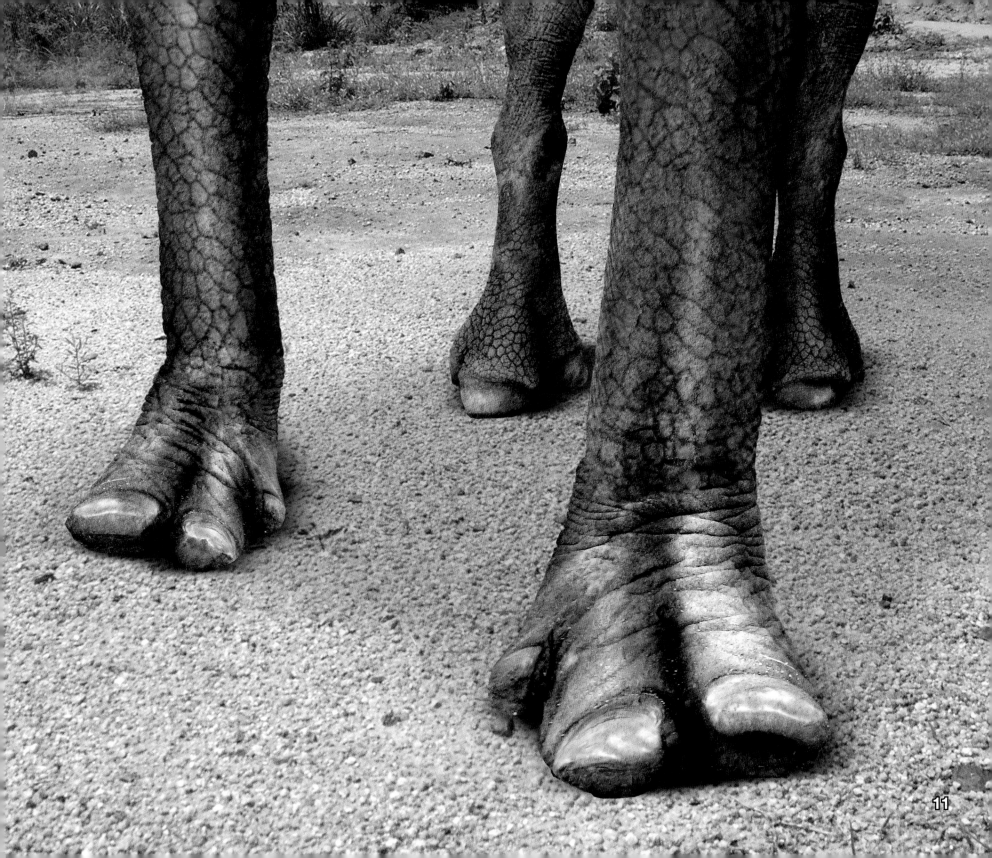

Giant rhinos had
very long necks.
They could reach
the tops of tall trees.

# What Giant Rhinos Did

Giant rhinos ate leaves
most of the day.
They used their strong lips
to grab the leaves.

Giant rhinos pulled
leaves from trees
with four long front teeth.
They chewed their food
with their flat back teeth.

Giant rhinos may have
lived in small herds.
They kept their young safe
from predators.

# The End of the Giant Rhinos

Giant rhinos died out
about 26 million years ago.
No one knows why.
You can see their fossils
in museums.

# Glossary

fossil — the remains or traces of an animal or a plant, preserved as rock

herd — a large group of one kind of animal

hoof — the hard covering on an animal's foot

mammal — a warm-blooded animal with a backbone; female mammals feed milk to their young.

museum — a place where objects of art, history, or science are shown

predator — an animal that hunts other animals for food

prehistoric — very old; prehistoric means belonging to a time before history was written down.

# Read More

**Goecke, Michael P.** *Giant Rhino.* Prehistoric Animals. Edina, Minn.: Abdo, 2003.

**Goecke, Michael P.** *Woolly Rhinoceros.* Prehistoric Animals. Edina, Minn.: Abdo, 2004.

**Riehecky, Janet.** *Giant Ground Sloth.* Dinosaurs and Prehistoric Animals. Mankato, Minn.: Capstone Press, 2009.

# Internet Sites

FactHound offers a safe, fun way to find educator-approved Internet sites related to this book.

Here's what you do:

1. Visit *www.facthound.com*

2. Choose your grade level.

3. Begin your seach.

This book's ID is 9781429600378.

FactHound will fetch the best sites for you!

# Index

Word Count: 137
Grade: 1
Early-Intervention Level: 16